Rectangular Morning Poem

books by Peter Ganick:

Two Space Six, Potes & Poets, 1982
Opaque Music, PostNeo, 1984
Lace Skeletons, Score, 1984
living beings, Xexoxial, 1984
sudden as pulse . . . , Score, 1986
Hyperspace Cantatas, Xexoxial, 1986
Remove A Concept, part 1, Pharos (New Haven), 1988
Braids of Twine, Tsunami, 1989

Rectangular Morning Poem

Peter Ganick

Potes & Poets Press Inc, Elmwood, Connecticut. 1989

for Carol
with love

This poem was written during September 1981.

ISBN 0-937013-27-7

Cover by Robert Moorhead

- 1 -

th pattern of a doorway
you see it nearer & nearer
th concerns from outer
taken inward to outward
to expressing th noise factors
that you like it
skimping on wishes
virtues a slant-roofed temper

when push comes to shove
alerted to re-group
third notions complete
    th fabric
you with outside
temperament cozy time
hot laughter from th group
again th objections
to talk more & less

- 2 -

what you hear in
    th evening
a lucky discovery of
    token feelings
wanting th situation
a conceptualized desire
what initially is its
    desire?

that which eliminates
   fear & longing

it is a cloister from
   a group structure
hermetically obtuse
comparisons of style
sizes of what is
   unaccountable

th support sequence
some thoughts thought
   in haste
arriving there saturday
longing from that day

– 3 –

needing good cheer
there is friends &
   free speech
a starter in her sex
anything that listens
   in fabulous disarray

it seems to go from here
alignment to a caterer
what th women want
how much is shows
   yr mind

what is liking solitude?
tails & nails
going thru emotions
th divine tuning
asleep in thought-forms
some color of support

once is necessity
a caged exterior
   tho thinking
listening to tension

– 4 –

attired by untruth
something reminiscent
   of yesterday
what is is there for
   all time
likelihood of belief

an intolerant nerve
everything in sight
th returnable path
as much as is curious

seemingly unending
coast-line carolina
downstream maine
a hardy flowing linear
   follow-up to greet

time put to use
see it as a lifetime
yr choices startle
   th certain discipline
some shot-up worlds
   where you count

– 5 –

ten fingers
ten toes & in hers too

some local society
commands from th queen
you are again at a situation

th world is a fish-bowl
you see thru th lens
    of perception
check on you
yr muscles that lift

perhaps more stringent
wet coffee & cigarets

th marathon simplified
a book of worlds & times

freedom th elixir
so much such that you
    can appear
told of th foundation
expecting reality

– 6 –

    from a magic touch
th auto was levelled
    into spoken
    eye-contact
you skip th sky-slot

heaven an emotion
what's there you are
    tricked again
th motives wear out
some complicated
    complacence

th time from you
    to you
it is nerves never lost
taken from strange places

th music thought & art
licorice likes th light
some helping necessary
helpless female role
    without you

- 7 -

surprise to see worlds
both sides yet
how much is emotion?
a how much? too for

so as much as spoken
show no fear
silence like mercy
what is heard?

th discussion is dance
    tho stifled
more tolerant
    because its heart
    is full
what ready forth
    th attitude

youd unify had there
    been silence
speeding in six hours
shots of demonstrative
    reasoning
known to that which

needs time
somewhat sleepful
something for many
    persons that can know
what you feel
where you look

sense & space-time
think & image
notions that are
    apolitically motive
    to reality

noise gone
a machine flutters
    eyelashes
studying traditions
worlds are used up

resources hang into th
    smallness awoken
what is asleep for now
however lately
    learned thru time
finished topical nursery

what accepts is another
    silent ocean
spree in th rocks
you glimmer from afar

th motion crawls thru
    copper pipes
smoke & smoke
drink & drink

th porch dog
some other greeting
third to be tired
    or strained

lips there known for
    itself nervy
obliged from an
    early start
no money to spend
    in th city

kept in hands folded
a curse that thinking is
    without itself

– 10 –

some book ideal
tho it is livable
unspoiled temper
stronger & stronger
aligning from
    that which is
    unlimited

youve developed this
    fluency to make
    it difficult
scratch scratch
voices on th slumber road

how you can speak
    in th night
sleep over
there is morning
    for slowest sizes

some inward motive
that which learns
    you

illegible & what it will
   call itself
from th harbor to
   th park
a sham dimension

pushing th fiery ones
lest that silence
cricket-filled

some filled-in bucket
so much alike
call thru for her
here to be away

talking newspapers
th societal model
this seeming longer
th cute top & bottom

a canister of urgency
saying for doubles
taken off th day
   instructed
a leaving thru beauty

tho it doesn't show
   it will shine
yr time span is indeterminable

what goes down
knowing to try it
some ear-shot leftists

were you once jealous?
a kiss brings back life

one's heartfelt needs are
  put to work
reign & th duo
some talk it frees

lessons in flowers
closely windowed as
  it takes away
  once egoic needs
likely to react with love
having it really heard

some night of it
somewhere to sit down
metal harness encouraged

– 13 –

as tho you are freer now
you so you now
did you notice that
  nothing happened?

cough in pierced eyes
hands blur objects
serve from conception

hot dependence license
  to hurt
why cant people
  treat others with kindness?
what you hurt is you

how yr concept flames greedily
cannot cancel a must

yr lucky notion
  found it well
certain extensions
families that ask

everything & everywhere
some book of detail
excumberating that
   noster
      silent morning
some portent
in a new light

stretches more th blend
   that ever-seeing
very quiet & this too

pearled cricket hum
to say of itself
after knowledge

out there an ending world
where habit becomes regularity
tho or another
th silent pen moves
th hand given
   is eternal beginning

something
you were here
   beside no depth-fall

only calm shimmering
   from th ocean
th flame from a candle

wherever & what why
   seems music
   tenaciously

automatic intensity
very surly
so as to feed

take one
   for yrself

– 16 –

will for new talk

will for circumstance

will happens

because you dont
want claims
in th future

what's expended
what's expressed
tho unlighted by th
   undisturbed sleeper

hey mo
now & some

new orleans
new orders
signifying all

if you can sort
   all th variables

– 17 –

some other primal potency
each cold rule of nature
   heightens awareness
   tho of ego

th first show with much to gain
from alone to diluted
delivers sopping trials

medieval-luxury-generator

you saw it before
   it hid on you

some craned neck
   wont find it
you are twice-careful
   in all you do

- 18 -

because it is
   new breakfast
as far as th eye goes

before th passion sets in
flakes of generation
th out-there
in-there

sequent to india
you hear of cities
that is as you
   for what's dialogue

trines & squares
how often? & how much?

is that it it all?
from where & how?
in roomy inquiry

from something less used
favorable inclinations
takes not with
anything unneedful
    or strange

something is itself
for
as long as arriving
takes a traveller's check
this sigh for no student

something you project
    reveals th symmetry

listen to outer
starts outer
starts inner
because it wont move   .

if it were a static
    awareness
having th force of a
    hydrogen bomb
contained within th brain

what she invites
    th cosmos
to visit at her door
would you budge from
    scenes that invite?

yes truth is one
sages call it by
    various names

something
of perhaps of
why she invites

– 21 –

because there's room &
light heartedness
there
how by
form of
much momentum

to language in that
soft intensity for
one who forgot th rules
talks about sleep

gathering in th
small wood
for th operations
inner heart-mechanism

does not praise
does no promising
knows to leave what's outside
outside

– 22 –

another remembering journey
yesterday

outer input
inner output
or shut up   all
th canvas
sincerely was taught to

rescue retired limits

in general
   all th factors in th play

lila that pleasing sound
one other from
   th other
subject — object
you take th collective
   opinion

see to take it
   with a grain of salt

– 23 –

some slamming door
interval in room

walks off in concern
soon

th world on a fast slick
invite that incursion
   which was
      thought about

surprisingly to act
   from mitigated beats
flexible rotunda
street corner peace

that acceleration-
   ritard variable
nowhere so obvious
   as constant remembering
   of th goal

rooms then
hits with reality

a spiritual experience
& needing so many
    variables
to keep track of

something devotion
salutation something

in a smaller world
precautions &
complications
never happening because
you take no extra
    baggage

& you have it all
from embarrassingly
    frank discipline

which unknowing force
takes th energy
    slight eye-closed
    a further shore

th soul in dimension
    lurking thru th turf
seldom very

very selflike that
    is th first impression
not to fly away

well used
used welcome
th perfect second-hand
  guest

alive in th gut
quest for whatever is
  let go within
    has no bounds

– 26 –

am flowing shapes
you elicit is & is
some basic freedom
then th hearing

heart-song out to you
th inner must show
  th wayfarer
  as an old tempo
trying to go forward
  within th
  all-pervasive speech

th talent of mystery
it's address is future
prepared in meditation
looking for nothing
  special

– 27 –

has opened a scam filed
  a brief sought a
  suit tho inconvenient

because & because

parallelled by mercy
something beyond
a soft horizon

labor day tangents
when you can look again

thought's opening
    is radically remembered
    is an utensil

until is inevitable
    as perfection is
    a poet's dream

– 28 –

something in th blue
    machine is
tho unformably there

something
            soft &
    full of challenge

something waves from
    th vibrations
that infernal clutter
where are you
    in yr mind?

restive for accumulation
restless from confusion
there is a spiritual
    basis
to everything th
    finding of it

some tearing into
  sleep
some reduced silence
  factor
something without
  looking at it

th contracted tickle
try years of mouths

some intense far
  away from you
some brought with
  an idea of happiness
leaving it at that
leaving with th
  differences
some more profitable
  activity

like lifelike & sincere
a blend-demon watches
  thru walls too

th atmosphere
  environment from
  th ultras pushed aside
not forgetting
  virtue & intensity

drive into th dark
a red-hot input
some iridescence
manacled to th spirit

into his surface
draws out th message
some sorrow applies
th context

– 31 –

even better music
from chance
from happenstance
to it
all coming to you

very out there is to
be no stranger
friends from th group
some differences
implied as tho
frequented th inner
consummation of core

one two three forms left
in daytime that
exploits whatever
whomever &
whenever

– 32 –

as when walks away
a photo & th ride

th crude message for
morning
sighs & breaths

moving from dark to light
in pursuit of

all infinities
          some glimmer
          of yoga

th system applied to
12th house pluto

stars & signs &
     mystery & growth
bent into a face
into an energy
     failing nothing

it is in mind
     like that too

– 33 –

some times
     are abstract
when where what
     are identifying
     factors

th monastery in th heart
that which makes clear
     sailing
unencumbered maya

you sail th skies
     & higher
some there from need
some see it all
     th way thru
     over th planes
     of existence

creation
maintenance
dissolution

quiet room
white ash
never perfect
but perfected

th diamond
th spare spade
th speak-talk connexion

ready to go
some week these here

you are inculcated
& you are love

said to inner sounds
that which freed you

because daylight is
    hampering
th reading of th music

behind that which is
    variable
    is a force
formations that are
    engendered back
    into consciousness

th unsurrendered
    perception a cause
    of reading th music

some distance yr frames
    have that input

free for response

vagaries of language
    & mind
not any more secure

- 36 -

because th activity
    answers itself
    without need for
    shining stars
or
    shy mascots you
    are uncharitable to

from as far as six
    hours to counting
    th use employed
or
    some young energy
    to you in expansion

th scorpio — leo link
variable lifetimes
awaiting th waitress

that which frees you
that you are from it

which shortens
th names of god

- 37 -

some open coldly
    without heat
it is a parcel of

straight-think

it is th tee-shirt of
th name of god
some open motor
chugging th fog

seeing a cricket
where th energy
started from

accumulation is what
hands make for
motives
their unsurreptitious
vacancy is as old as
to wonder

– 38 –

where there is no name
where shadows freeze
where forests clear out

when th difference
when attacks accede
tacks in rows

many sitter
babes in th open air
that they are to ask

to free any dome
lift levels
th bevelled patchwork

concept reconnaisance
cosmic joy knows
love's you

thought must have a
deeper foundation
than anything before

what's awaited is life
what you kiss for saint
th noise & th late hour

a task in morning
longer as it is here
& it is not heard from

beautiful from energy
th world's all illusion
knowledge of th
  inner significance

getting later at sooner
no response is
no responsibility

totally aware
as you are aware
to yr own capabilities

double-tongued
you need to seek clearly
has always to say

has leo thought-fixed
  rotors
teaming up with
  th enchantress

thru response

not fear
th meditation in
  before & before
  after

you seek it straight on

there are
            many

– 41 –

maintenance of
  free consciousness
types of snares
  all
  rooted in maya

you dont mind
  giving it away
  to th stares of
  friendly strangers

eliciting th combinations
  that free mind
  to self-inner
  awareness

saturnine
saturate
endure
lose all   (to
get all   rent
brahman
direct
  approach

winding down
  before energizing

peace in th air
getting sleepy from
  up

her utensil
  creates th hour
some city
  would like learning

meditation before
  coffee
carol asleep
  after th input

no signs of weather
  tho th sky is dark

letting it hear
from one sound
  all are generated

words too have
  one genesis
creator of life

two people that
  can decide
th motion towards
  inner propulsion
  inner perfection

as it goes this

forth in decency
in th hour of
one's heartfelt need

- 44 -

you find
in-motions &
tensions
without adequate light

a few days outside
another day
this day
carol in th bed
awoken to touch

tho you are undone
you know realms that
recreate th energy

outlet in th car
first in th sack

something
reminiscent of
not going away

th heart is a
leprechaun

- 45 -

a giving of love-energy
that to which is
confidence & what
you wait on it

dinner for refined egos
no fear from those egos
  that maintain th
  tempo

where there's resistance
  to th fortune
  judging with
  two pairs of eyes

you seeking there
  tides truths
  for another side
  of this lifetime

– 46 –

these patient books
awaiting to be real

burning piles of hitler
th south
alexandria
  not to call it
  faster than
which excepted
  from wanting
  til then
  but

  what watches
  all this
  is th sequent of
a dynamite idea

sounds like you
washing   walking

that which is momentum
very suitable
& realistic
& money-making

rather organized
   & in another plane
   & in a free concept

designing th alternating
   of dualities
such that
   these are th world-choices
   for this lifetime
   in th hidden house

wanting to get protected
th excitement of
   th first city
laborious week silenced
labors that you are
   her

held tongue behind
   teeth in front of
   teeth
tongue of th gods

there is that reversal
a dimension plus
   concentration on
   th goal

- 49 -

because it is morning
& youve noticed all there is
in th natural silence

sounds by halpern
afloat into th cosmos

any time th 2nd world
likes to listen to being
in all its complementary
    motions
            something you saw
a woman's & man's love
th clout to take it right
    thru to th unknown
                    that
    vision you see th world
    you live with

- 50 -

hand-held world you
you
you therefored rightly
    & in its heartfelt
    emotion

seeking inspiration
you
you & her howevering
    nothing is into
    sight here

there's universes to defend
crusades taking flight

    that organizes like a

cluster lights a smoke

they-lit from universes
    that lifts and alleviates
    cosmic guilt
th french & th english

- 51 -

a desirable focus
a darkness
a variety of distraction

something you discard
an energy of removal
an atmosphere of
    acceptance
  something for yr
    anglings thru
    pronomial litter

living in her life
you hear a difference

there is a spiritual
    approach
that is th link
saw from public family
to th work of th
    blanket to
    keep warm

- 52 -

& because it's so
there's always

there is no mention

of
& because it's
   mistaken identity
   is forged

never never never
then voices from
   th past

you that insist
you every non-worry
clothes for th concept
favors from th gods
then public family

& because there is so
therefore a stranger
   turns friend

- 53 -

some paternal
   maternal
      incompleted
   to therefores
      & controls
   varieties
   limits onward

   limits to link
      left alone
   from th scarlet
      to th bronze

can recognize
transcendence

can live it
every day

assigns th multiples
for political benefit

– 54 –

th owner-energy
an om let into
   th atmosphere
blessing that one
   carries on for a
   wild & straight
   force in dealing
   with it in public

time-sense plus th
   five others
isnt there even one
   sense that is th
   sixth, that of
   sensing time, th
   fourth dimension?

are aware
   silent
   go on
      in peace

– 55 –

when perhaps by excess
th blurred fantasies
congeal th truth

wise as therefore
thoughts diversify

so much like wisdom
th peace & light

of anodized steel
fabricated from th
   walls you conquer

that theatrical news
for ego is a denial

yet th statement
you refuse that notion

               it is
beyond ignorance
               it is
a facility beyond
   th flux

– 56 –

some unchanged energy

th serpent assigns
   to privacy

cantankerous & kindly

cake that slices
   yr life

if youre going to
   tap that many

six week old dashboard

dreams in th context
   of practice

some reason you
   hold forward

like th emotion
   attatched to you

bend a ring thru
  consciousness

concept: retraction to
  inner

functions that choose
  no other safety

28 hours &
  seen an armful

for a second time &
  th group th first
  time

when in convention
  or conviction about
  a certain object

retraction of worlds
concepts that free
a poem without
  advertisement

you protect virgo
you are moon-sun
  combinations

truth & reality
  beyond mind-echoes
nothing than hardly
  asking to be excuse

simple little
  four-letter word
next to th fireplace
  in thanks heard

in th faces of
   who do you mean?
th face that listens
   to you

- 59 -

some sentimental
   all over th places
   on floors of
   a growing ideal

now softer
now idly for
   ten dollars raise

hearing senses that
   you talk softer
retiring into
   retracing one's steps

some authentic motion

to & for rest
to & for life
to & furnishing
   th broken cage
   for th space

- 60 -

th sound that
spirit defeating illusion
as an ever-deepening
   experience

th form a multitude
   of confrontations
th link in notations

& labels

something from th
   other side
a version to being
   what one is

there is no sideways
   motion
th fractions invent
   th polls

– 61 –

sift   (ego gratias
concepts
for accuracy in
   a truer vision

trowels in th earth
it feels like strength
therefore oppositions
   & what you clear throats
   to delineate

infractions & to hope
   to breathe thru th
   reality as a little
  bit shot in an universe
   reserved for filling all
   vacancy without shouting
   that energic expansion

you neednt be
   stranged by th
    prior moment

some hasty
  delvings will
  reveal th
  immenseness of
  further
  inner structures

prominent among th
  new items
  objects indisposed
  to hide what
  teaches within a
  space of solitude

a personable sect
  that has no
  ultimate
  foundations to
  crack

develop a mind
"one two three four
 & fifty millions"
th child counts aloud

paring down
  th necessity of
  loving th bright light

understood &
  delicate understanding

that spring-time
  year round

that recollection in
    an interface with
    intuitive aspects
    of language
unless you try to
    find out meanings

– 64 –

walking into one
    light
one motion
one cause-effect
    relativity
one cute tension
one light interval
    sharing th coffee

editing th news
addiction to her love
mercy on th
    shelves where
    you equal 8½

th film designer
    watches th hours
    to zeno's following

th hours forever
    expanding
    th realm of
    a cautious heart

– 65 –

a knot of expectation
    winks at inner forces
    seen in a summer night

th attraction of looking
& saying before th interval
does a sort of schizophrenic energy
on what talkingness
of mindstyle is revealed

on it in th door
transcendence
wipes th feet for
clearing th green
before ignition

– 66 –

subject – object
of an intensity
how you know inner
delvings
what you say to
th neuters
you prize that activity
you infer is courage in
facing & disciplining
th unknown without
a usual drive for power

knows th arbitrary
th pulse of a universe
inventing all other ones
whying th necessity
can be a devastating
experience in ego-revision

as long as in this plane
as long as thoughtful options
do many things
at once to suggest
where thoughts arrive
in multiple oceans

- 67 -

this is extraction
    of a small density

for time to think
    of inner harmony

a miracle a minute of
    harmony without
    regret

savoring th peace by
    helping it consider
    every silent vritti

dualities &
    th forms of language

tripled polarities

quadruple spaces

infinite additions

- 68 -

with th search
twice or once
nearer & it's
    three hours
    that invent
    th cosmos
busy as
resting as
transcending
    forms
            because
    therefores
    are cute

also
timelessly urgent
a rectangle is
    sought
what we'll do
    is an avenue
    of exchanges

– 69 –

th most beautiful
    was life th
    unplanned
    aspects & th
reality that holds
    you here

carefully arriving
    in th all-season
    city
    nothing & everything
    is planned for
    oblique fathers
    of wayward
    conception

at th house
where we grow
something pushed
    up in another
    form for entry

– 70 –

where you take it
where you go for it

take to go for it

give form to hours

you see a process that
  hassles & reneges
  before commitment
no apple purse
  is more or less
  concentrated from
  those hours
                in
limbo   another
traction
        would
having it been
from th heart

- 71 -

that a person is
able to seek much
from talking

desiring that which
escalates th options
fraught with twin poles
  of sorrow & joy
        in th morning
th hustle
        youd be
surprised however
arrangable yr
mutable serpentine
listenings
        any
functions because
now it's thought of
& hearing something
familiar tests th
endurance

one afternoon anon
    with gallant
    merriment

slip thru th motion
some external closeness
    to an energy
    of life &
    spiritual fulfillment

burns down to
    something well
    liking not too
    therefore-jargons
    you assign to
    each relative pit

thru grace &
    preparation for grace

utensils
relax & create

winter surely comes
    to understood
    relations in time
    found & blessed

held hostage to love
    for what big cook
    liking to cook
    a true & pure love

for th new start
    feeling infinity

as th dream of
harmonious
inflections   th world
behind a mutual karma

– 74 –

not to ask task skate
willing world-dharma
when associated a
    having time

for th beatle
    arrangement
energy shared is
    energy saved yr form

material interception
anything unseen
our lady
    on happy tricks
    of illusion

our maya
    unshattered becomes
    bygones in th
    pest of a
    past attachment

– 75 –

saw it once
a twisted pain
neutral
        plus or minus
evaluation of
    inner care full of
    silence

th creator
at harmonious desk

stricken thru some
eastern energy

if she likes it
she will

famously anonymous
inner freedom
attracts
inner freedom

- 76 -

you can shake sounds
from a salt-silo
th result habitated
th world
it is aware
you couldn't destroy
ego any faster

a burnished torch
finds a likely
refutation
result of
quick communications

awake
some illusion
of hooks & bars
freed for awake

another phase
varying th realities
    creatively
knowing how it
    sounds thru to
    th non-temporal

something like an
    echo of forms

thicker silences
you sing th song
th song sings th life
it has always been such
    because it is true

likely to this song
a pronounced difference
    tween referent &
    reference off-time

gaining grist th delicate
    balance is best
    not thought about

still never
a placard tossing
    th grand entrance

some sweet sweeper track
some not so pleasured
    & later it curves thru
    that dimension so
    fully understood
& complains as formality

hearing as tones
it is background for
    reporting complete
    transmission
    transfiguration
    transcendence
    transnational
    transits &
    transient

terror avoids
    this heart

– 79 –

because one
doesnt notice
everything
            one is
            specialist
            on one wavelength

th invitation from
    acceleration
                th deep
cut
    normal relations
    wholesome pastimes
cut
    flames perpetual
    as wind & stars
cut
    nature because its
    love is so beyond
cut
    an illusion tho
    only as far

– 80 –

sleep for work
  for sleep works
to regenerate &
  give one instance
as prodded to excel

where was night
  when we needed it?
how did timeless silence
  invade our hearts?

something strange &
  something familiar
th round shot
  something fearless
something silent

– 81 –

th premise of that book
that which eats yr palm
  before entering
some dairy glue
  from sequent
  awareness

redone & uncaged
  th morning knows
  its circuits &
it is freedom sought

– 82 –

that wants you

that needs affirmation

thruout options

that couldnt say

that you were there

that it watches patiently
    of th second person
    of inner-out brought
        to a focus

because this starts
    an emotion
experienced & passionate

not letting free
trying to hold for
    eternity

some eyes in th
    iota of discernment

– 83 –

food is not to be
    disturbed

th vibrations must
    ease th sensations

th aetheric element
    must remain pure

one must experience
    much disturbance

to know th value
    of peace

th one customer
th twoness bedeviled
caring about th depth
  of music

nothing in this world
liking & licking
again venus in scorpio

th fragrance of love
its names & forms
  defy cynicism

to elevate what
  likes to listen
greening of th
  pentagram

some blonde quality
  invites fun
invites hourly
  minutes

a lot of
  experience

something to extend
  to where nothing
  has crossed th path

there was a
  general silence
  while fading
  during vacancy

sounds & delights

music soft or loud
some roller not here

cruller consciousness
women as free birds

delight in th gazelle
    rushing th territory
    in africa

names & forms
all are unconscious

– 86 –

because there is
    crossed opened &
    sniffed
        clover that
    understands some
    fascination

not on a verbal level
tyranny of th media

self-reliance
    & self-resources
th rectangle of
    decision

you see th forms
    in th snakes & cats
once saved
    believes in god

some things of her's
    in my pocket

– 87 –

unknown &
  full morning
tells us th secret

tell us of blind
  karma &
  its effect on
  meditation
  while alive

because you see
  th evolution
  thru th training
  of memory

what is his
  experience of this?

th return & shout

joy & laughter

some spiritual
  dimension

– 88 –

there is th material
  structure
not knowing where
  it comes from

replicate freedom
  & place
rain shining of
  th streets

some people behind

some ahead

th seriousness
  of conversations
a life for you by you
  & of you

something for
  virtual infants
attached to no thing
  from or to

you read as if you
  were gone

– 89 –

because th energy
got complicated
certain instructions
were not followed

out on th street
there are no warm
happenings beside
devotion & joy
  of being

youd not have
surprises
except that
no one told you

– 90 –

something in th ecstacy
  of ordinate items
something unfulfilled

even th surprise
a blessing on those
that think

at her mother's day
feed
therell be another
because you say
th other is th same

th different &
walking thru
variant light
intensities

confusion of arrival
a soft morning
between two rivers
in there
for a card

as a problem
for working thru
sleep-alertness
factors

colors th morning love
given th advanced
notation
stones in th city
crowds since seven p m

assuming th best
foreign soils in th feet

under th dust
it is quite clear
of manifestation

because after
tho must mucho
  obtain
much must relate

create lazy luck

it is an honor
  ego decides as
  on worldliness

with th magic
  of denser fields
  forthcoming
done itself th favor

creatures of
  morning cities
  in every city
  of all th citizens

denizens of
  opportunity

some with difference
arranges sky sounds
  likely th motives
  arrange th motions

closer to core-reality

to-dos about tankards
  options closer
  therefores
you check it on
  a certain scale
  of values

what means th mercy
was th is of
  now & forever

– 94 –

when that april
arrives again

  seek it everyday

th sagittarius
  connexion
arrows in th stars
piercing golden fruit
letting light
  spread its fingers

to something
  shiatzu
severalling afterwards
  after completion
to something
  finding th sun

a lamp of its own
  concentration
  retrieved

– 95 –

some long morning
  with immanent
  phone reflex
  determined

th mind watches
  th mind
  every time it

sleeps for
acceleration

cause — effect
th hello in every
   tongue
         creates
   a million feelings
   of excitement

at last count
   crowding th future
equally obtuse

– 96 –

a saint & a seeker
this lifetime it is

th answers of
   th flesh
mindlike & sincere

dramatic for holding
   on
however for
   remembering
   that
   ever-growing
     space
is th rule of love

– 97 –

for as unfinished
   furniture for when
          you
   read it again

transmission of
variables
a new transformation
when you
recognise it
all alive with
th sport
th flight internal

with assigned
struggle
it
builds you

you-saying
therefores
th new
synthesis
equally as
radiant
conversation

something touches
deep in
rangeless
territory

that th new form
is souls recognised
assigned th values
in a longing
before it gets
its way
with you

space between
   space   akasa
th merciful context   .

frames of a lamp-post
   lit within th core

understood
   then emotive of
   ideas
       whittling
   down th whistling

no music out
th 3rd floor meow

silliness
   very too apt to
   trick theatre into
   obedience

for one motion
   disguised &
   distant from

watching infinity
   grow thru
   lights from

harbingers of
   improvisation
   seems long from

heterogeneous
   subtleties you

swim in from

th wind

- 101 -

family concerns
   like disorganization
   like retractions
   like flaps on
   soft windows

inside
   dont let on
th noose
   that itches

neck-surround
it is different
   so it is a
      discipline

- 102 -

fun at th roost
herein th blameless

you see it arrive
younger by a magic
   totally within th
   concept-desiring
   of maturity

keeping busy
keeping thoughts
   above th anchor
   well beyond
   th flaked
      oceans

– 103 –

whatever you see
th fourteenth
    combination
should wake th afternoon
    defined
rolled into town
one purr plus

how it works out
    that to order
    th verbal vagaries
stuck with a
    large impression
    of inhumanity

forty large henna-motes
clusters in thought's eye
every 200 miles
    some
spiritual context

– 104 –

no close play
    terminates without
    laughter
                on
    or off
            pushed thru walls
            was th
    excitement beyond
            th frame

where it is experience
    not to look
    yet to see thru
    th management

with a special
  activity-constraint

– 105 –

something
somethink
  elsewhere-thoughts
  some other fashion

creative thru nineteen
  verifiable intentions
  only for th love of it

not to tone down
  th lights
special thanx to
  th lights
every incident reminds
  th lights

a cross word
  escapes to return
gets free
  gets free

– 106 –

with schedule
  & intensity
    requiring several
    imaginations in this
    hot-headed city

a chance operation
  with mucho
  cancelling frames

th disguise for
  what looser
  creates joy
where hard to find
where until there
  were no
where energy weeps
  for what had
  tender to be

– 107 –

coats & cities
star thru night
th fusion radiant
some nights are tried
  for th sake of it

restoration when
revolution now
worlds that sting
a bottomless level
  horde of goals for it

that which equals
  all intentions
  before it

as a collapse or
as however th picture
  relives it

– 108 –

in an eye
for th regard

third eye sensitivities

large fluid overwash

antennae of an ant
swatches of blue mercy

totally ascribed to
    developing th
    requisite arm
        movements

taking to th kids
published lethargies

th requisitiveness
    of an ant

– 109 –

a charger thru
    greeting   some
                        two
jewish blossom
places   six years
indeterminate time
    tells one what
    to focus on

there is an innate
    freedom
    in th choices

longer
softer   hangs th phone
slower

was as is what wanted
    not to feel far
    from th four hours
check

some flood of child
watching th worlds

– 110 –

without disturbance
stare   stare

duel yr older factions
challenge th
   emptiness

totally unvoid with
   subliminal
   expertise from
   kosher subconscious
   impulse
refuted for th
   handy microphone

where heaven is
   lying beside
th poetess from
   th frame
   from th forming
   of such allegiance

– 111 –

reaping th inversion
   of change
its colorless chancy
   operation
where you see it
   change
into th highest reality

awakening to silence

outer & inner

as a seduction immanent
    joy
th moist pattern of
    excess
joy & longing for ones
    who exist

creators in th density of
    what is not apparent

– 112 –

as all is illusion
monday   monday
doesnt fear th reaper

knows th friends
from sunny sky
beautiful people

beautiful person
as all is love
that intenser smile

& if it were all reality
    to be so real
    we'd must th
    signifier of
    egolessness

– 113 –

without concern
without blind
    indifference
that which looks like

th other
having a book of
    reminders

strengthening th discipline
you are glad it is
    this morning
ahead is th future
it is one day at a time

every vedic opportunity
th life flows & scowls
    behind th ears

deft dumb silence
unpatronized
    not from
    straight ahead

– 114 –

there-willings to
    be fantastic
    immersion
will will will
thereby th struggle
    to defy gravity

music is life
life is a blend
    of musics
you define yr ego
    to ascend into
    greater dissolution

catching
    upward-moving
    energies
is that all there is?

how small is big?
how big is
    th high high sky?

– 115 –

something that pulls
    you back
something th morning
    knows of you
    for th decision

following space
    into hidden &
    interminable
    existences

have yr freedom

retain yr freedom

there is no unworthy
    attachment
there is th language
    of approach
everything is a
    self-conscious
    worldliness

– 116 –

for isolation
    engenders
    th older forms
    of death

                you
bring it skyward
to tell from

a satellite
of wishful memory

song that lives
    freeing hearts as
    yr painful illusion
to turn to today
    youve thought
    about it

today tho it is today
th life-light
    of all serenity

– 117 –

one sentence from
    another's intensity
    as an
all-wish for solitude
    yet others

enforced discipline
    thruout distractions
    attending
    thought's delivery
    it feels with caution

even if it is even
if there is
    no measuring
    th density of
    a love-offering

hand that links
    form to form

– 118 –

something afar
  noted for other

th jupiterian
    occluded by
  saturnian impulse

some women
  is lesson-learning
you can perfect
  yr spirit
  in work after
  th boss has
  dropped off

wish-love
everything as much
yr slice of island
  into th atlantic

– 119 –

because of their faces
because ego is
  out to lunch
because you at times
  dont like like
  what's seen

as another level
  th crowded
  exception in th
  farmland
rehersal space

as another rising
  will of dualistic

effort reminds ego
of its urgency
on a string
wherein that is
culling no favor

- 120 -

now's th time
now's th option to
    face it
within these forms
    you are reunited

destined worlds
    ego escapes
freer th two &
    romance &
    steadiness in th
    pedestal

something needing
    itself
no between

targetted remembrance
    of healthy
    concentrations

th dying by loving
th infinite
    reservoir

- 121 -

because instead
because infinity
because all those days

had no
because

not letting becoming
assign other than
spiritual values

small beady-eyed
black silence
on th street
in roxbury visioned
variable slaughter
like serving today

a daytime good luck
that resolved
by grace
no knowing
those forms

– 122 –

so it is part
of th field
you present
a circumstance
of th bucket
disturbing no one
in that which
sleeps & speaks
as you say it

because there is
so little to ego
it can lose itself
readily
circumstance
to circumstance
form to
form

th crucified
nirvana-approach

– 123 –

awaiting th silence
motives of
   morning stretched
to take a visit &
   pray for th reason

for breath in
   furtive destinies
climbing a damsel
   forced by
   inner pressure to
   you that get it
      back

before th imprints
   have settled
restful mind
   in new hampshire

left it there
   for those
   immense
   polarities

– 124 –

once is alternate
   delivery

th assignment to
   talk to
th faces &
   th face
   of a crystal

unknowing stasis
before th
  said & done

window rockets
october
no plans ahead
  for th life inner
  fear calls thru
  to face reality
  & face that
  without fear

- 125 -

yr pretending further
  no further
  than you can jump

putting inner necessity
  to look-see-think
to put it here
  as tho she is
  in a nearby room

yr curiosity
  invites sagittarius
after finding out
  a kiss of facings
a silence
  totally inner

blushing to hold it
  freely afloat
some gossip notwithstanding
  outsiders fan hopes with

because it is
  still th same

nightly laughter
& joy

– 126 –

because it is approach
fanning th flames
    of exhibition-halls
changing for th
    tightrope

where rest arrives
    in th weekend
to play alone
    she is not alone

every romantic nuance
th role of what
    is found there
to beam thru
    th noisy water

held shows for
    protection of
that which finds
    in another
something you are
    for ego

– 127 –

some isolated
    terminology
implicit mind
    & focus
temerity from time

a woman's world

a man inner thru
  to her
to seek wisely

some congratulatory
  askings
then phone tables

critical impulse
  dropped a level
impatiently &
  wanting patience
  now
& then a further
  application

– 128 –

what is th notion
you have egoed with

however strange

however simple

  something from
  a chart

any from as th
  dimensional flourish
24 hour openings
  because it starts
  as morning

that which seeks
  its options

as it is fearlessly
  shorn
      th man is
in blues while
  regarding
  th circumstance
  projected for
  tuning in on
  reality

a new spontaneousity
  linked rumor
  about th
  menial coherence
  talking to
  th optimum rock

th karma of a scene
  at handing you
  there already a
  polarity in
  forming th climate
  of th telling

with a serpentine outlook
  sting sting til crash
  predetermining nothing

        equally reality
        equally as much
  as you there is no
    forgetting
            th urgency
of yr appeal

fictionally artificed
is ego calling things
   & plots
        work for

even semirealistically
   as much
   option-forming
   greater pictures
   thru modesty
   says th changes

   as you are a
   finalist in
   recruiting where
   you can be
   anonymously
   adventuresome

seeing
   that person

carol
for you
th ocean
slips into
gear
    a mountain inner
   a river outer
these are notably
   recent realities
     because somethings
   are reflected back

& also in discrimination

to elevate her heart
th little girl
   under th press
combinations that
   love you

– 133 –

form-facing
   th form-faced

four faced
   several connexions

fourth level
   a witch of
   th curate

designated survival

someone everyday
clipped stutter
      talkful

what inside attracts

what outside objectifies
   primmer than
   white cats
      in th sunshine

– 134 –

sometimes somewhere

om shanti

   that rolls hills
   to hills
   tho cosmic apartness

thinks to rejoin

concommitent on
    inner-outer
    relations

very regular only on
    a little late
seeing from what
    becomes health

– 135 –

th world is
    boundary
    after boundary
where's th free access?
where do foreign soils
    take th longest
    to sing praise?

evaluations
expectations

enemies of energy

th with which you
    are free
    because one is
    reminded

valueless & precious
toned-down motion

green   far green

– 136 –

th line of energy
    is a psychic fact

give take
  talk quick
    approaches
      something
        beyond th fact

th mediums of
    exchanged brokerages
talking around th
    hours
      when you come over

that old projection
this new dharma
    no escape
    from
    innate freedom

– 137 –

oh free bird
oh where are you from?
how have you arrived
    here
      at this forlorn
      & desolate vision?

provoke & dissent
    when appropriate

th rain is cold
    when passionate
      is here is there

elder gossip &
    cthulu-rodents
    & masks of secession

just this week
    start all over

th aging & poignant
destiny

- 138 -

that which
    disembodied spirits
probably respond
    to

with & with
it is every world
there is softening &
    pacifying

strong & brilliant
    in a patience
fought with
    th argument of
    combinations
reasons than
    th inflamation

royal hectic
    shroud of a
    momentary
    passing

- 139 -

this is th direction
    from imitative
    mondays

images of finesse
    suave svelte
combinations &
    connexions

as asked
& started
   into th
   business talk
before which
   it was infinity

– 140 –

before optioning
th cake & eat it
scene th foremost
   progenitor of
   any half-wit
   neutral

ashen face
dead to that life
   was one th rule
   formless ego

icing on th toes
some shiatzu maiden
   catching a cold

– 141 –

as th time
one before th other
   before th other
      before th other
   etc
was more mantricly
   available

from exact schedules
   two hours no 36

seeking it th which of

notoriety parlayed

clara says
    like is a great
    racket

– 142 –

you are once again
you are
            there was
a defused magic
inner to there
                that which
was perhaps will not
or would be
            so as much
commonsense it
seems to want to
aid
    into th structures
    behind th
        structures

when &
such

– 143 –

because are known
    from quarter
    in th storm
unsettles as if
    notationally
    impossible

when & is something
    future is & that

was running to you
was fortressed with
    faith & knows links
    between forces

love long severe ego
capable of
    directed choice
    magician's impossibility
    that is nowhere

th striated leprechaun
    responds to
    a higher notion

– 144 –

was & by yr will
then look into faces
then create th lesson
then & thensome

how truthful it is
that there nods into
sleep in th quiet
then & thensome

difficulty expressed
two faces & no other
two become one onward
then & thensome

was that not delight
in pinpointing th
ecstacy?
        a drama from
energy of start
energy of maintenance
energy of continuity
energy of controlling

th mental waves
then & thensome

– 145 –

in formless faraway

now & then
a tear for all other

is it is
watch you sting back

th highest option
carefully planning
    th reasons
that which summer weight
    can get mouthed
    after a month

seeking it here
havent missed it else
from variation
encircled harmony

now & then
eternally

– 146 –

when for effect
  there disorganized
    interrelations tween
    truth decided &
    truths determinable

are very level &
    into competence
    one or two

ahead
that permanence
arranges for th moments

that selects
to fix blocked
outer ferments

that a
dissection would tax
intentions

that frees
th response

– 147 –

places
all of than which

people
all of than which

is th only rule
two truncated arpeggios
noises from that ocean

going on
over where there is
that than which

as on basho's
exertion watching
for foursome friendful

– 148 –

where you were
simplified amidst
this sea of

                    complexity

          whether on-mind
                    off-mind

          whether there is an
               emotive expression
          amidst this
               largo entity

          sui generis
               from organic reeds
               serving this
               fascination
               to entire worldlike
               options

               levels realms
               universes
               freedoms

          back to school
          friend   friend

          – 149 –

          hold onsets fiercely
          to total that wearing
          th rink-watchers
          th ring warmers

          it is not
          but yet however
          but however when
          yet however so not

          distractingly logical
          formless out there
          there was never too
          being a frame
          following into

what which with
criticism

is better bravo
to live to it
severing all
prior claims

– 150 –

find you here
th silence aware
    & populated

corrections on that which
    poses entropy

for every
for any
    scene into th maze
    correctible on that
        which invites

beckoning rudely
    & still th decision
    is made

for chance
for change
for that which
    these as such
    implicate
    verbally

– 151 –

alone with th moment
    you seize is yrs

a duple-metric obtains

no finality

rolling thru space
    just as determined

long long years th
    sky was high for

one hundred camels
    in th courtyard

never again th
    one hundred camels

wearing this soul is an
    expertise of tails

one for two or zeno
    where numbers shine

light thru th window
    reminds th hour

fasting th driveway
burns

– 152 –

th war zone
th restaurant
    is a scene
wow-pops in tanks
omelet friends too

multiples
    see to go by
    into what is
    into this that
    which into is
    th form of th
    computations

no from soul

there's a titled
arrival & th
hours less
than ten

– 153 –

from motion
   some fuzz
on a brain

archaic barbarians
noises of consolation
appearence of
   whatever development
   wonders th brain

for you from motion
   archaic holiday
turmoil for
   some months &
   mouths to feed

able to contemplate
silent is th world
   for it
large talk
hysteria
notable service
   brain

– 154 –

tiled picadors
subrelative nosh

creep & fly in
   yr rule

cheer & flan in
therefore until
which when

as logic as frame
as automata
concrete blessing

about th blessing
say th roads
learn
paths

– 155 –

fear understood
what worlds
where was
zap with eggs
a cutaneous
chloroform bath

identities in arrangement
of surprised
by ecstacy

some forms herein
when you talk
twelfth house

exception you something
a fare in th backseat
dimensions that
prove that innocence

let here into
yr facing reality

some love
softer than brilliant
   outspoken news
   outheard th music

cheerful intention
formless because
   track record

improvident tasks
   mercies &
   follow-ups
   at th backing into
   miser-fixtured
   arrivals when
   it is to see
later

something th ching
   says what to do
   you seek?

current askings
   reasonableness

flourish stand-stills
   tho you dont seek it
something right on
some other thing
   some other thing

from space acrimonious
   completion
   safety of mercy

no pitfalling seeing

pitiful in th
static starlight

you are here

– 158 –

ignored to
experience each
moment as
faraway th
week goes
so slow

withouts from
turnarounds from
melody & harmony

    tunes this
    cosmic soul

blessings
    ego derives whens

later you accept
    th involvement

– 159 –

some looks th ocean
    floor of being
hazy skies
forms thump creases
options sift
    thru open hands

some movie motion
    escalates when
    she is from here

taught in th silences
   & their internal
   maintenance

moon in earth
corporeal fantasies
   carry overland
   that which as
   much as for must
   provide more than
   idle complacency

– 160 –

starts to decide
   th myth
logo of th archive
interpreted faces
   as toward you

seen from silence
   ego blankets th
   onslaught often
   formally inspired
yet no delivery

interpreted faces
   you toward th
   sky
      into whatever
   larger
   than a life
   larger than
   imagination

th extension of
   boundaries
   in time

some inclusive asking
not for self
           means to
a spirit moves
  nickels & dimes

clear colorless

blank faceless
  therefores
until life refers

some life
before youd
  accomplice
  for noises
some far dream

something silent
  & present deserve
  density   force
  & silent sleep
    gift triad
there equates
  what in force
excels for what
  is night niceness
& therefore
& also blind intuition

worth
    smile
hardshipping
    th heart

handicap in
　mantra when as
it
　　becoming
ledge a
　　portion of
it's all
　　too munched

　grinning ear
to sky with

POTES AND POETS PRESS PUBLICATIONS

Susan Howe, *Federalist 10*
Janet Hunter, *in the absence of alphabets*
P. Inman, *backbite*
P. Inman, *Think of One*
P. Inman, *waver*
Andrew Levy, *Reading Places, Reading Times*
Jackson MacLow, *Prose & Verse from the Early 80's*
Barbara Moraff, *Learning to Move*
Janette Orr, *The Balcony of Escape*
Maureen Owen, *Imaginary Income*
Keith Rahmings, *Printouts*
Dan Raphael, *Oops Gotta Go*
Dan Raphael, *The Matter What Is*
Dan Raphael, *Zone du Jour*
Maria Richard, *Secondary Image / Whisper Omega*
Susan Roberts, *Cherries in the Afternoon*
Kit Robinson, *Up Early*
Leslie Scalapino, *clarinet part I heard*
Laurie Schneider, *Pieces of Two*
Gail Sher, *w/*
James Sherry, *Lazy Sonnets*
Ron Silliman, *B A R T*
Ron Silliman, *Lit*
Ron Silliman, from *Paradise*
Pete Spence, *Almanak*
Pete Spence, *Elaborate at the Outline*
Diane Ward, *Being Another / Locating in the World*
Craig Watson, *The Asks*
Hannah Weiner, *Nijole's House*

Potes & Poets Press, Inc.
181 Edgemont Avenue
Elmwood CT 06110